THE LEGACY OF GENGHIS KHAN:

BARBARIAN OR REFORMER?

Mina Gavell

Alphabet Publishing
www.AlphabetPublish.com

The Mongol Empire
- at Genghis Khan's death in 1227
- at its greatest extent in 1279

Genghis Khan's name brings images of violence and war to mind. During the 13th century, he and his Mongol army left a path of destruction from Western China to Eastern Europe. So why are modern scholars, and even the Pope, praising him now?

Who was Genghis Khan: Violent barbarian or brilliant reformer?

INTRODUCTION

Genghis Khan was one of the greatest military leaders to ever live. He began his career by first uniting the Mongolian tribes into one nation. From there, he went on to conquer parts of China before heading west. By the time he died, his kingdom stretched from Korea to Hungary. It included much of China, all of Central Asia, and parts of Russia. His sons and grandsons expanded the borders to include Persia and much more of China and Russia.

The people living under him spoke numerous languages and all practiced their own religions freely. Genghis Khan set up the first international postal system and restored the Silk Road. The Silk Road was a trading route that linked Eastern China with Europe and the Middle East. By improving the infrastructure and protecting those who traveled on it, trade and economy throughout the region increased. This also allowed ideas to move more freely between the East and the West. Some modern historians claim that the **European Renaissance** would not have happened without Genghis Khan.

Nevertheless, Genghis Khan is not usually included in the lists of great leaders such as Alexander the Great and Napoleon Bonaparte. Genghis Khan is more likely to be found on a list of villains. For many, his name is **synonymous** with terror and cruelty. After all, 40 million people died during his invasions.

Who was Genghis Khan really? Was he a great leader who brought order to the world or a cruel murderer who brought death and destruction? Can both statements be true?

Introductory Questions

1. Have you ever heard of Genghis Khan and the Mongol army?

2. What do you know about the Great Silk Road?

3. What are some of the features of modern society that you value?

4. Why might some historians choose to present only one side of a story?

5. Can violence and force ever have a positive outcome?

CONTENTS

CHILDHOOD YEARS

The origin story of the Mongol people is grand. They were said to come from the mating of a wolf and a deer in the high peaks of the Khentei mountain range. However, the early years of Genghis Khan were not. In 1162, near the Onon River of Mongolia, a baby was born to a woman named Hoelun. She had been kidnapped from her own tribe, the Merkit. According to legend, this baby was born holding a bloody clump in his hand. For a long time, this was the only sign that this baby named Temujin would one day become the great Genghis Khan. Temujin's father, Yesugei, was the leader of a small but tough group living in a camp along the river. Some historians claim Yesugei was noble, but this seems unlikely as he did not rule a kingdom and lived in simple conditions.

Alleged Birthplace of Genghis Khan

Until the age of eight years old, Temujin lived a humble but

The Onon River

6

comfortable life. During this time, he met Jamuka, a boy who would be both his best friend and later, his fierce enemy. He also became engaged to his future wife, Borte. The Mongol custom was to get engaged at a very early age and marry as a teenager. However, Temujin's father was poisoned by an enemy and died. The family now had no adult man to provide food for them and protect them. The rest of the tribe saw them as a burden.

One night, the tribe took everything that belonged to Temujin's family and disappeared. When the family awoke, they found themselves alone with almost nothing but the yurt (a traditional Mongolian tent) they had been sleeping in. The next few years were very difficult as the family survived by gathering nuts and roots, fishing (which was not considered respectable by Mongols), and trapping small animals like mice.

These years were extremely challenging for Temujin and his family. As the family worked hard to survive on such little food, the tension between Temujin and his older half-brother,

TRIBES OF THE TIME

Kereyid: located mostly in the center of what is present-day Mongolia. Temujin had strong ties to them as they supported him when he reclaimed his kidnapped wife, Borte.

Jurched: located southeast of what is present-day Mongolia. They are also known as the Jin and are associated with the Manchurian tribes of Northern China. They were not farmers, not nomads.

Merkid: mostly located on the northern border what is present-day Mongolia. Hoelun, Temujin's mother, was engaged to a member of this tribe and living with them when kidnapped by her future husband, Yesugei. This tribe later kidnapped Temujin's wife, Borte.

Naiman: located in the western area of present-day Mongolia. They were a very powerful rival of Gengis Khan before he defeated them.

Tatars: dominated the eastern part of present-day Mongolia. They were defeated by the Mongols and spread across the empire. Tatar communities can still be found in Russia, Central Asia, and China.

Behter, grew. Temujin was frustrated by his older sibling's bullying. He was also aware that Behter would one day be the leader of their family—and even have the right to marry Yesugei. So Temujin and his younger brother killed Behter with arrows. Finally, Temujin was showing his strength—and his violence. However, his difficulties were not over.

Not long after, the family was attacked by the Jin tribe and Temujin was taken into slavery. As a slave, he had to wear a wooden device around his neck and hands that prevented him from feeding himself. He had to rely on the help of others for his most basic needs. Luckily, he was able to escape during a celebration. While he hid in the woods though, a soldier found him. For some reason, the soldier felt sorry for the young boy and brought him back to his home. The soldier's family fed

Temujin, removed the wooden device, and gave him a horse to escape on. Temujin never forgot this kind act. After he became

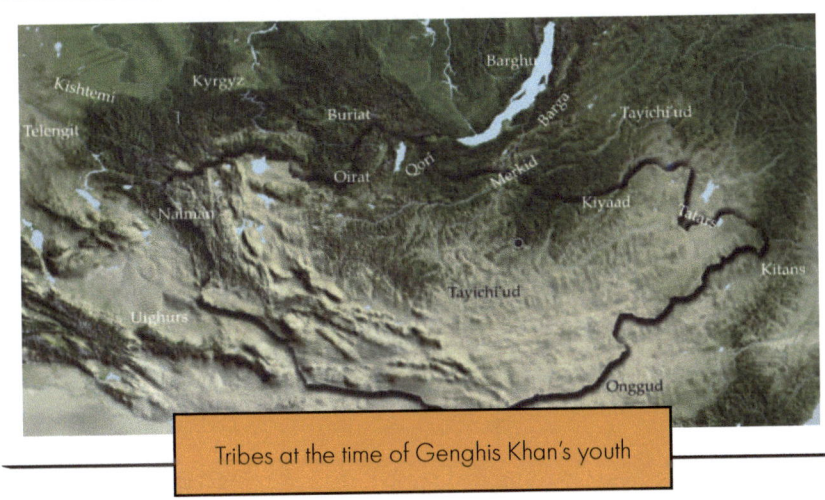

Tribes at the time of Genghis Khan's youth

powerful, he returned to reward the soldier and his family.

Now back home again, Temujin looked forward to a calm and peaceful life. He and his brothers were now older and stronger, so they could provide a better life for their family. At last, Temujin could marry Borte. But again, things would not go easily. Soon after the wedding, his mother's tribe, the Merkit, came for revenge. They kidnapped Borte.

BECOMING A LEADER

For some historians, this marks the beginning of Temujin's change into Genghis Khan. Fighting to get Borte back forced him to make partnerships with neighboring tribes, including his childhood friend, Jamuga. Once the Merkit were defeated, and Borte returned to her husband, there was new respect for Temujin's clan. He also had a better understanding of his own abilities. In fact, soon after, he was declared Khan (leader) of the Mongols.

Temujin probably hoped this new position would allow him some peace. Yet, as he grew stronger and wealthier, he became more of

Genghis Khan Exhibit

Temujin named Genghis Khan

Inner Mongolia Museum

Genghis Khan and Borte

a target, even to those who had once been his friends. Before long, Temujin was fighting battles against his friend Jamuga, as well as other tribes on the steppe such as the Tatars and the Naiman. Luckily, during this time, Temujin also gained many new friends and allies. Many of the people he defeated were inspired by his actions and battle and afterwards joined him.

At this time, the usual custom was to kill all one's enemies or make them into slaves. Temujin was different. If his enemies promised to be loyal to him, he protected them and made them part of his own kingdom. Another way Temujin was different from other leaders of his time was that he did not only reward his friends and family. Instead, he gave money, land, and other gifts to anyone who helped him, even enemies. When he defeated an enemy, he looked for skilled laborers and engineers as well as those who could read and write, and gave them positions in his army and government. The soldiers in his loyal army came from many different tribes and religions including Buddhism, Christianity, and Islam as well as Tengriism, the religion of the Mongols. At that time this was very strange. In fact, Jamuga is an example of someone who followed the traditional practice of rewarding only his friends with treasure and high positions. He was also famous for his cruelty, even boiling prisoners alive.

In 1204, after many dramatic battles, the final fight between Genghis Khan and his former friend Jamuga happened in the Altai mountains. The Mongols were victorious, and Temjujin was officially declared Genghis Khan (Universal Ruler). Jamuga escaped, but was later betrayed by his own soldiers. Genghis Khan executed these soldiers for their disloyalty. Some historians say Jamuga was honorably executed, but others disagree.

CONQUEST

It seemed that at last Genghis Khan could finally rest and enjoy the fruits of his hard work. However, now that all the soldiers of the steppe had become one large army under him, he needed to keep them busy. The Mongol people had also become accustomed to the wealth that came with success at war. So, for about the next ten years, Genghis Khan led his army to fight people north near the Siberian border, into Northwest China to conquer the city of Yinchuan, and against the Jin Dynasty in Northern China to capture Beijing.

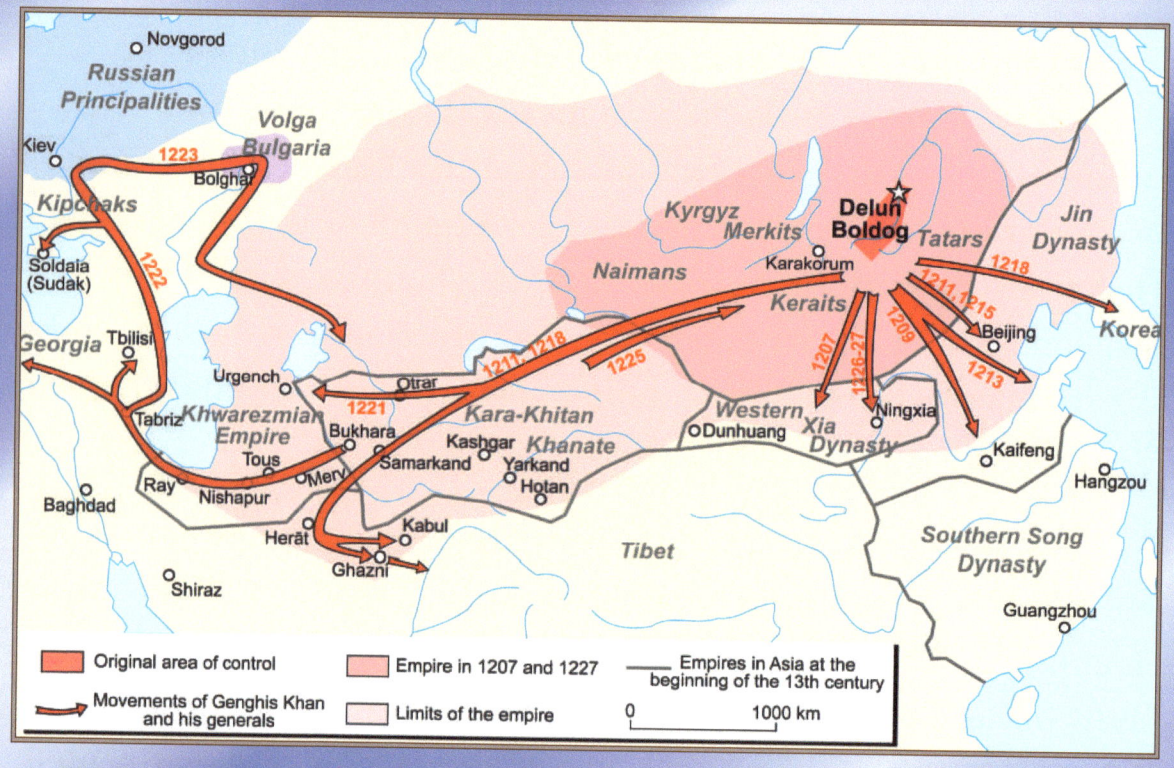

▬ Original area of control	▬ Empire in 1207 and 1227	── Empires in Asia at the beginning of the 13th century
➟ Movements of Genghis Khan and his generals	▢ Limits of the empire	0 1000 km

    With all his own steppe people fully loyal to him, and the surrounding areas pacified and paying taxes, Genghis Khan turned his attention west toward Central Asia and its Silk Road. At this time, all luxury products such as silk, spices, and precious metals moved along this trading route stretching from the Middle East to China. With Europe still in the dark ages, Central Asia was the center of culture and education. During the many successful battles over the years, the Mongol people had developed expensive tastes. The best way for Genghis Khan to make his people happy was to make a deal with Muhammad II, who ruled the Khwarezmian Empire of Central Asia, and much of Persia and Afghanistan. Muhammad II, however, was suspicious of the Mongols and their plans. Genghis Khan sent diplomats to Bukhara to meet with Muhammed II, requesting a trade deal. Muhammed II's reply was to kill the diplomat and many of the merchants traveling with him. He disfigured others before sending them back to the Khan. For Genghis Khan, this was one of the worst things a person could do. Mongol society always treated diplomats well, even those from their most hated enemies. Revenge was necessary.

CENTRAL ASIAN CAMPAIGN

In 1219, Genghis Khan led 100,000-150,000 Mongols to the gates of Bukhara, threatening to destroy the city if Muhammad II did not surrender. The Sultan refused and kept himself and his armies behind the high walls of his city. Though he and Bukhara were safe for the moment, this allowed the Mongols to roam the rest of the kingdom attacking the other unprotected cities.

Meanwhile, Genghis Khan set his engineers to work building weapons designed to break down the walls of Bukhara. Local people were offered protection if they surrendered and joined the Mongols. Those who didn't were killed and their bodies were used to fill the moats around Bukhara's walls.

In 1220, Bukhara fell. It is the only city that Genghis Khan set foot in. He did not like the smell and feel

Genghis Khan giving a sermon to the people of Bukhara

Alleged symbol of Genghis Khan

Coin from the Mongol Empire, early 13th century

Decree plaque of Genghis Khan

of many people living in a small area and usually left his armies to finish the work in the cities while he waited with the horses in open fields. Maybe because Muhammad II's treatment of his diplomats had been so offensive, Genghis Khan made an exception for Bukhara.

Not long after, Muhammad II's home of Samarkand surrendered. Genghis Khan sent his sons throughout the rest of the empire to finish off any remaining armies. This led to the Mongols' first encounters with eastern Europe. It also resulted in the destruction of three of the world's greatest cities of that time—Nishapur, Merv, and Herat. Descendants of Genghis Khan continued to spread north and west from this point. They also created the Mughal Empire which built the Taj Mahal. The city of Bukhara remained a Khanate ruled by Mongol descendants until the Russian occupation in 1920.

With Khwarazm now part of his empire, Genghis Khan considered exploring India, but soon realized the climate was not suitable for the Mongol army. Their horses required cooler, drier temperatures and large areas of grasslands to graze on. Instead, Genghis Khan turned his attention back towards China. He returned to Western China for his final campaign against the Xi Xia, who were not following the agreements made with the Mongols previously.

DEATH OF THE KHAN

In 1227, as the Mongols were about to win another battle, Genghis Khan fell from his horse. Though he continued to fight for several months, he was unable to recover from his injuries and he died on August 18th. This is one account anyway. The explorer Marco Polo reported that the Khan was struck by an arrow. Other historians think he died of disease. Regardless, his body was buried in a secret location near the sacred mountain Burkhan Khaldun. His son Ogedei, who was the most reliable and well-liked of his sons, became Khan. Though the Mongol empire soon broke up into different kingdoms, the descendants of Genghis Khan continued their growth. At

The Death of Genghis Khan, from *The Travels of Marco Polo*

Modern military: While the Mongols used the ancient Roman structure to organize their armies, they made many improvements. Membership and rank in the army was based on ability and hard work rather than one's position in society. The Mongol army also had a dedicated medical unit to treat and look after injured warriors. Most importantly, the Mongols used a sophisticated communication system that allowed their forces to change and adapt strategies at a moment's notice

Gunpowder: Gunpowder was invented by the Chinese and used in weapons that burned slowly. The Mongols, however, experimented with gun powder and changed the recipe. The result was more explosive and could be used to fire cannons and guns.

Siege machines: Early on, the Mongols struggled to defeat walled cities and fortresses. But over time, their engineers developed siege machines such as catapults that were very effective. Most importantly, they could be built quickly and locally rather than traveling long distances with the heavy equipment.

The Mongol bow: The bow used by the Mongol armies was much better than those used in the rest of the world. It was lighter, more accurate, and could shoot further distances. This allowed them to shoot deadly arrows against enemies while remaining safely out of range.

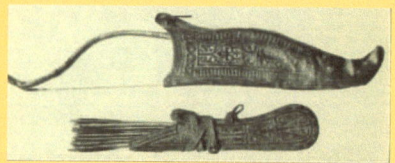

Stirrups: Though the Chinese are believed to have invented stirrups, the Mongols popularized their use and perhaps introduced them to the west. The use of stirrups was one of the reasons that Mongols were such skilled fighters on horseback.

Block printing: This was also invented by the Chinese but spread westward by the Mongols. This technology allowed for the printing and sharing of paper money, administrative records, all types of informational documents, and even playing cards.

Paper money and standardized currency: As trade was essential to keeping peace in the Mongol empire, paper money was popularized and insured by the government. The Mongols also used silver money that had the same value in all areas of the empire. This allowed for easy currency exchange, rather than having to trade physical goods.

Postal system: In order to send information and messages quickly across their huge empire, the Mongols created the Yam system. It was made up of a network of relay stations that provided fresh horses and riders to allow written messages to move continuously without delay.

their height, Mongols ruled from the Sea of Japan to eastern Europe and much of the Middle East, an area of over 9 million square miles (23 million kilometers).

Centuries later, the fame of Genghis Khan and the Mongol Empire remains, though mostly in a negative light. Genghis Khan and the Mongols have become symbols for cruelty and violence. However, for the last decade or so, historians have been reviewing what we know about Genghis Khan from various sources and changing some of their opinions. For example, the Mongol's reputation for loving blood (and even drinking it) does not make sense according to what we know about Mongol culture and religion. For Mongols, blood was taboo; the sight of it was offensive. Their preferred fighting style—shooting arrows from a distance—kept them away from seeing or touching blood. In fact, for a Mongol, an honorable death was to be rolled up in a carpet and either suffocated or stomped on by horses as neither the blood nor actual dead body would be seen.

Looking at such facts has even caused some historians to completely reverse their view of Genghis Khan. Rather than a violent barbarian, they see the Mongol leader as one who brought progress to both his own Mongol people and all those societies he came in contact with. He brought peace to the people of the Steppes and greatly increased trade throughout his empire through his policies and practices that ensured safety and structure. Many historians argue that Genghis Khan created the conditions for the European enlightenment and thereby, our modern world.

Illustrations of horse-hair standards used by Genghis Khan, called *sulde* in Mongolian

The Mongolian Empire at the time of Genghis Khan's Death

Kirgis
Burjat
Taijut
Solang
Birat
Merkit
Mongol
Tatar
Liao-yang
Kerait
Karakorum
(Residenz 1220-1257)
Naiman
Önggüt
Uigur
Kan-su Tangut

LEARN MORE

"10 Things You May Not Know about Genghis Khan", History.com: https://www.history.com/news/10-things-you-may-not-know-about-genghis-khan

"15 Facts about Genghis Khan & His Legacy", The Collector: https://www.thecollector.com/genghis-khan-facts/

"Genghis Khan", Encylopedia Britannica: https://www.britannica.com/biography/Genghis-Khan/Legacy

"The Rise and Fall of the Mongol Empire", TedED: https://www.youtube.com/watch?v=wUVvTqvjUaM

STEP INTO THE STORY

The year is 1215. You live in a city somewhere on the great Asian Steppe (the land that stretches from China to Hungary). A year ago, Genghis Khan swept through your city with his army and claimed it as his own. The city now belongs to the Mongols and the people of your city pay taxes to his nomadic army and government. What are your memories of that day? What is life like now in this city so recently taken over?

When you think back to that day, do you see images of barbarians "thirsting after and drinking blood, and tearing and devouring the flesh of dogs and human beings" (the first words written in Europe about the Mongols). Did you see blood in the streets? Did you hear the screams of battle and the crying of people losing everything?

What do you see now? Is the city in rubble and ruins? Are you starving from hunger and paying taxes to the Mongol ruler who now sleeps in the city palace? Do you wonder how you and your city will ever recover from that fateful day?

Or, is the situation quite different? On that day when Genghis Khan and his army rode through the gates of the city, was it your city's own army who opened the gates? Were the soldiers who died those who disagreed with your own ruler's decision to surrender to the Mongols? Does the city around you look better than before? Is there more trade with near and faraway cities? Before the Mongols came, maybe you and your family practiced your religion in secret. Do you still? Are you and your people free to practice in the open now? Has life improved?

For hundreds of years, many historians presented this first, violent image of Genghis Khan and the aftermath of the cities he conquered. But in the last decade or so, many historians have been looking deeper and closer into what we know about the Mongols and presenting a more positive version of their impact on those they conquered.

Which one is the actual truth?

THE THEORIES

1. Genghis Khan and the Mongols were violent killers who destroyed many cities and communities. Not only did they kill millions of people, including innocent civilians, they did so with great violence and cruelty. They can also be accused of committing genocide, as they sometimes tried to kill off an entire group of people.

Historical records show that when Genghis Khan attacked an area, many people died. Some historians believe that there was an 11% decrease in the world's population as a result of the wars waged by Genghis Khan. That's roughly 40 million people. A census conducted in China during this time shows that the population dropped from 120 million to 60 million people. Similar statistics were recorded in Russia and Hungary when the Mongols invaded those areas. When the Mongols took over Baghdad, over 90,000 people died. Many of these deaths were direct results of violent fighting, but many more also died later from hunger. It was a common strategy for the Mongols to destroy farmlands outside of cities in order to provide more grazing pasture for their own horses.

As for the violent and cruel nature of Genghis Khan's fighting style, there are many tales that support this theory, particularly during the conquest of Central Asia. We have already seen that Genghis Khan had such little value for human life that he used the bodies of people living outside the Bukhara to fill in the moats so the soldiers and their carts could cross easily. Generally, during the Khwarezmian campaign, the peasant class was only valued for how they could be used against their own armies. Before attacking walled cities, it was common to increase terror in the surrounding towns and villages. This caused the general population to stampede the protected cities adding to the chaos and terror. When attacking Bamyan in northern

Afghanistan, one of the Khan's grandsons was killed. In his rage and grief, Genghis Khan ordered his soldiers to kill everyone, including dogs, cats, and chickens.. While this was extreme, it was a common policy upon seizing a city to execute all soldiers and aristocracy. Unlike his European peers, Genghis Khan saw no added value in the lives of the rich and powerful. He did however value skilled laborers and craftsmen, seeking them out and offering them his protection in exchange for their loyalty.

The above example of Bamyan also supports accusations of genocide. We see this also in the campaign against the Khwarezmian Empire in which the Persian population dropped from 2,500,000 to 250,000 people. Today, very few people know about the Western Xia culture of China because its people and cities were so completely destroyed by the Mongols.

2. Genghis Khan and the Mongols actually improved life for many and set up conditions for our modern world.

On becoming the official ruler of the Mongol people, a population of over a million people, Genghis Khan saw the need for official rules and policies. One related to the military was the policy of awarding pensions to widows and orphans of men killed in battle. Enslaving people who surrendered to him was also banned. Instead, the defeated could join the Mongol army and be successful if they worked hard. In addition to military reforms that encouraged people to be loyal to the Mongol nation, not just their own tribe, many social changes were put into effect.Another was to outlaw bride kidnapping, perhaps because of the violence and conflict he himself had witnessed as a result of both his mother and Borte's kidnapping. Torture was also outlawed. Religious freedom, as mentioned, was also guaranteed to all people under Genghis Khan's rule and protection. Moreover, most cities that were defeated by the Mongols quickly recovered and grew their economies due to their inclusion in the new trade routes. Technology such as block printing and the use of gunpowder arrived with the Mongols, as did the use of paper money, a dependable postal system, and diplomatic immunity. Taxes tended to be moderate rather than burdensome. All nations that declared allegiance to Genghis Khan could govern themselves for the most part as long as they paid their taxes and their laws did not conflict with those of the Mongols.

Though Ghenghis Khan may have been violent, he was no worse than others of his time. Compared to the violence committed during the Crusades, or by the Persians or Chinese in their wars, or by Tamerlane in Central Asia hundreds of years later, Genghis Khan's acts seem normal and perhaps even tame. During the campaign in Khwarezm, there were many stories of Mongolian violence. However, over time, Jallaladin, the son of Kwarezm's Shah, Muhammed II, gained a reputation for being even worse than the Mongols and to his own people. And in terms of numbers of victims and cruelty, Genghis Khan does not compare to more contemporary figures such as Stalin, Hitler, or Pol Pot.

Some historians argue that many of the stories of Genghis Khan's violent nature are either exaggerated or unfairly blamed on him. In fairness Genghis Khan himself was responsible for some of the exaggeration. As a person who understood the value of reputation, Genghis encouraged people to spread wild stories about his cruel and violent soldiers. Frightened cities often surrendered out of extreme terror before the first arrow was fired. This was the case with Samarkand after Bukhara was captured. Moreover, many of the exploits attributed to the Mongols occurred after Genghis Khan had already died. For example, the terrible destruction of Baghdad happened over 30 years after the Khan's death. Often, historians have also mixed up Genghis Khan's actions with his descendants or his generals, blaming him for each and every act of violence and destruction.

WHY DOES IT MATTER?

The legacy of Genghis Khan is a story that belongs first and foremost to the people of Mongolia. Yet, for most of history, other people have told the story. For example, much of what we know comes from Marco Polo's descriptions or from people who were conquered by the Mongolians. During Soviet times, it was forbidden to speak of Genghis Khan in Mongolia. Now that such restrictions no longer exist, it is important for the Mongol people to reclaim their history and national hero.

This is important for the rest of the world too as we move away from a view of history that sees Europe as the center. Understanding the context of Genghis Khan's world helps us see that while Europe was in its dark ages during this time, human progress was not standing still. In fact, many argue that the Renaissance that marked the end of medieval Europe would not have come about without the influence of Genghis Khan and the Mongol Empire.

On the Pope's September 2023 visit to Mongolia to celebrate the growing Catholic community there, he praised Genghis Khan's policy of religious freedom and said it was the reason for Mongolia's long period of peace that followed his rule. In our modern world, where religious differences still lead to violence and war, the Pope's mention of Ghengis Khan is an important reminder that in some ways the world has advanced little. Whether one sees Genghis Khan as a villain, an innovator, or something in between, his tolerance of religious freedom should serve as a model to us all.

FUN FACTS

The word "mogul" is derived from Mongol.

Today, over 16 million people carry the genes of Genghis Khan. That is approximately 0.5% of the world's population.

The famous Kublai Khan was a grandson of Genghis Khan. Temurlaine also claimed to be an ancestor (though in actuality, he married an ancestor).

Visitors from both China and the West were shocked by how independent and respected women were in Mongol society.

When Genghis Khan rescued his first wife, Borte, after she was kidnapped, she was pregnant. It seems unlikely the baby was Genghis's. Nevertheless, he raised this son as his own and defended him against all claims that he was not the Khan's son.

Christopher Columbus, the explorer often credited with discovering the Americas, carried a copy of Marco Polo's writing in hopes of finding and meeting the Mongols during his travels.

GLOSSARY

aftermath (n.) — events caused by an event or the time after that event.

ally (n.) — friends or supporters; military allies work together against an enemy

barbarian (n.) — a person who is uncivilized or is inferior to others, used as an insult

devour (v.) — to eat in a very greedy way

disfigure (v.) — to ruin or harm someone's appearance

disloyalty (n.) — lacking loyalty or faithfulness to someone

execute (v.) — to kill as punishment for a crime

infrastructure (n.) — the basic systems that make a town or country work such as roads, buildings, public safety, plumbing, postal service, electricity, etc..

luxury (adj.) — expensive, beautiful, and/or fancy things

merchant (n.) — a person who buys and sells things, a trader

moat (n.) — a large hole dug around a city or building to protect it, sometimes filled with water.

nomadic (adj.) — not living in one place; nomadic people move with their animals according to the seasons

pacify (v.) — (*here*) to bring an area under control so they are not a threat to you.

rubble (n.) — broken stones and bricks particularly from buildings that have been destroyed!

suffocate (v.) — to die because you don't have enough oxygen to breathe.

surrender (v.) — to give up and admit defeat

synonymous with (adj.) — means the same thing as or is closely associate in people's minds.

taboo (adj.) — considered extremely rude or bad

tastes (n.) — (*here*) the kinds of things that people like

thirst (v.) — (*here*) to want or desire very badly

PROJECTS

1. **Write an essay or create a presentation**: In your opinion, was Genghis Khan a hero or a villain? Support your opinion with strong reasons.

2. **Research**: Look at the map of the Mongol Empire. Choose a country and research its relationship with Genghis Khan and his descendants.
   - Did the Mongols have a positive or negative effect on the development of the country?
   - How do the modern day inhabitants feel about Genghis Khan?

3. **Discuss**: As a young man, Genghis Khan (then Temujin) was captured and enslaved. He only escaped with the help of someone who felt bad for him.
   - What if he hadn't escaped?
   - How would the world be different if Temujin had not been able to become Genghis Khan?

4. **Debate**: Genghis Khan and Mongol soldiers killed many people and destroyed their cities. He also brought about a lot of progress and innovation that improved people's lives. Did he do more harm than good?

REFERENCES

Andrews, E. (2023, June 25). 10 Things You May Not Know About Genghis Khan. History.com. https://www.history.com/news/10-things-you-may-not-know-about-genghis-khan

Badwen, C. R. (2025, January 1). Legacy of Genghis Khan. *Encyclopædia Britannica*. https://www.britannica.com/biography/Genghis-Khan/Legacy

Beyer, G. (2024, April 14). Genghis Khan & His Legacy: 15 Facts About the Ruler. The Collector. https://www.thecollector.com/genghis-khan-facts

Broadbridge, A. F. (2019, August 29). The Rise and Fall of the Mongol Empire. YouTube. https://www.youtube.com/watch?v=wUVvTqvjUaM

McLynn, F. (2015). *Genghis Khan: His Conquests, His Empire, His Legacy*. Boston, MA: Da Capo Press.

Singh, M. (2023, December 25). The Mongol Hordes: They're Just Like Us. The New Yorker. Retrieved from https://www.newyorker.com/magazine/2024/01/01/empires-of-the-steppes-the-nomadic-tribes-who-shaped-civilization-kenneth-harl-book-review.

Weatherford, J. (2010). *Genghis Khan and The Making of The Modern World* (J. Davis, Narr.). [Audio Book]. Brilliance Audio.

Genghis Khan statue complex in Tov, Mongolia

ISBN: 978-1-956159-59-2 (print)

For permission requests, write to the publisher at "ATTN: Permissions", at the address below:

29 Milo Dr. Branford, CT 06405 USA
info@alphabetpublishingbooks.com
www.AlphabetPublishingBooks.com

Discounts on class sets and bulk orders available upon inquiry.

Cover and Interior Design by Walton Burns

Country of Manufacture Specified on Last Page

First Printing 2025

Images

background Flickr/Jasmine Halki CC-by-SA 2.0 • ii top Depositphotos/Furian, standard license • pg. ii middle National Palace Museum of China /Anonymous Artist, Public Domain • pg. ii bottom Flickr, CC-by-ND 2.0 • pg. 6 top Flickr, CC-by-2.0 • pg. 6 bottom Wikimedia/Chinneeb, CC-by-SA 3.0 • pg. 7 Wikimedia/Popo Le Chien, Public Domain • pg. 9 tribal info Walton Burns (Data source: Atwood, Christopher P. (2004) Encyclopedia of Mongolia and the Mongol Empire), CC-by-SA 4.0 • pg. 9 map Depositphotos/Zelwanka, standard license • pg. 10 top Flickr/William Cho, CC-by-SA 2.0 • pg. 10 middle top Wikimedia/Jami al-Tawarikh manuscript, Public Domain • pg. 10 middle bottom Flickr /Gary Todd, Public Domain • pg. 10 bottom Wikimedia/Basawan or Bhim Gujarti Chingiznama, Book of Genghis Khan, Public Domain • pg. 12 Wikimedia/ Ty3718, CC-by-SA 2.5 • pg. 13 Wikimedia/Ahmad Tabrizi, Shahanshahnama, Public Domain • pg. 14 top Flickr/Pia Andrews, CC-by-SA 2.0 • pg. 14 middle Wikimedia/Classical Numismatic Group, CC-by-SA 2.5 • pg. 14 bottom Flickr/Gary Todd, Public Domain • pg. 15 Wikimedia/Rustichello da Pisa, The Travels of Marco Polo, Public Domain • pg. 16 top Wikimedia/Diez Album, Public Domain • pg. 16 middle top Metropolitan Museum of Art, Public Domain • pg. 16 middle bottom Wikimedia/Rashid ad-Din Manuscript, Jami al-Tawarikh, Public Domain • pg. 16 bottom Flickr/British Museum, Handbook to the Ethnographic Collections, Public Domain • pg. 17 top Wikimedia/Metropolitan Museum of Art, Public Domain • pg. 17 middle top Wikimedia/Gary Todd, Money Shanghai Museum Coin Gallery, Public Domain • pg. 17 middle bottom Wikimedia/Cnanie, CC-by-SA40 • pg. 17 bottom AdobeStock/City Animal, standard license • pg. 18 both Wikimedia/Sci Show with Moh, Public Domain • pg. 19 Wikimedia/Hardcore Mike, CC-by-SA 3.0 • pg. 20-21 Metropolitan Museum of Art/unknown artist, copying panels by Zhang Zeduan, Public Domain • pg. 29 left Flickr/Francisco Anzola, CC-by-SA 2.0 • pg. 29 right Flickr/Francois Philipp, CC-by-SA 2.0

www.ingramcontent.com/pod-product-compliance
Lightning Source LLC
Chambersburg PA
CBHW041446120626
46547CB00002B/360